BALLOONS
FROM PAPER BAGS
TO SKYHOOKS

Astronomy balloon as seen from the gondola.
See page 42.

DESIGNED AND ILLUSTRATED BY THE AUTHOR
WITH PHOTOGRAPHS

BALLOONS

FROM PAPER BAGS
TO SKYHOOKS

by PETER BURCHARD

THE MACMILLAN COMPANY
NEW YORK

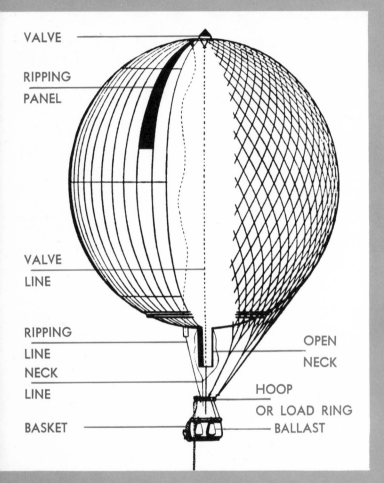

VALVE

RIPPING

PANEL

VALVE

LINE

RIPPING

LINE

NECK

LINE

BASKET

OPEN

NECK

HOOP

OR LOAD RING

BALLAST

Before the invention of
plastic balloons, this was a
standard gas balloon.

U.S. Civil War balloon.
See page 36.

Acknowledgment is made to British Crown Copyright,
Science Museum, London, for photos credited to The Science
Museum on pages 9 and 31; and to Science Museum, London,
for photos on pages 8 and 30.

This picture shows the
"Hindenburg" moored at Lake
hurst, N.J. in 1936.
See page 34.

AUTHOR'S NOTE

This book hits most of the high points of ballooning, but many notable flights are not mentioned here. Events like the flight of "Explorer II" to almost fourteen miles in 1935 and Major Simons' ascent to nineteen miles in 1957, though they were record flights, were similar in many ways to other flights described in this book.

My thanks to the Science Museum in London, the National Aeronautics and Space Administration, the U.S. Navy and the National Science Foundation for their help in gathering facts and pictures.

For their personal interest and help, my thanks go to Sam Holmes, who helped me get the book off the ground, to Dr. Jean and Dr. Jeannette Piccard, to Captain Kittinger of the U.S. Air Force and scientist Charles Moore, to Merrill Jones of General Mills, Inc. and Lieutenant Eaton of the Lakehurst Naval Air Station and Fred Zuckerberg of the U.S. Weather Bureau. Last, but by no means least, thanks to my childhood friend David Poole, who has always had an eye on the moon and the stars.

PETER BURCHARD

OFFICIAL U.S. NAVY PHOTO

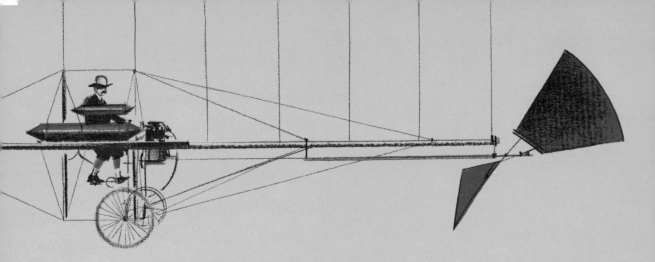

Santos-Dumont in No. 5.
See page 30.

CONTENTS

DREAMS OF FLIGHT

Before the invention of balloons, men looked up at the birds and dreamed of flying. Some, with wings too small for flight, jumped from high places and came crashing to the ground. The air around our earth was a mystery to them. Now we know that it is as real as the rocks and the trees. It weighs billions of tons.

This wood engraving of the ancient Greek legend of the flight of Daedalus and the fall of Icarus was probably the first printed picture of man in flight.

One of Leonardo da Vinci's designs for flight. Leonardo lived from 1452 to 1519.

A model of Francesco de Lana's design for a flying boat. The designer planned to lift it with thin vacuum globes, but the pressure of the atmosphere would have collapsed the globes. It was designed in 1670. Neither this nor the airship below was ever built.

THE SCIENCE MUSEUM

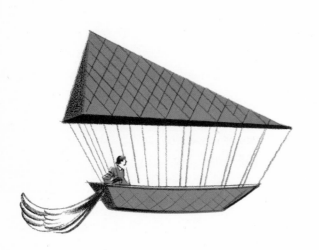

Gusmão's design for what was apparently a hot-air balloon or airship. He designed it about 1715.

9

PAPER BAGS

Joseph Montgolfier stood on a rooftop high over a street in Annonay, France. He unfolded something that looked like a sheet and a tangle of ropes. He moved toward the edge of the roof. Men gulped and women screamed and Joseph jumped. The cloth billowed over his head, filling with air, and Joseph floated safely to the street.

Joseph wished that he knew how to go up as easily as he had come down. He and his brother Etienne and his sister Marianne lay on their backs one day looking up at the sky. "Do you think we could capture a cloud?" asked Joseph.

Afterward, at home, they noticed the steam rising from a kettle in

their kitchen and they put a paper bag over the steam, but the steam condensed and the bag fell to the floor. Then they tried putting the bag over the smoke from the kitchen fire, and, since hot air is lighter than cool, the heat of the air in the bag carried it to the ceiling!

They made larger bags and heated the air in them by putting them over a fire made of wool and straw. The bags rose and floated away.

In 1783 they made the first real balloon. It was large but it carried no people. A crowd gathered in the market place to watch while a fire was built under the balloon. Men held it to the earth by ropes, and, when they let go, the people cheered as it floated into the sky.

MAN GOES UP

After the successful experiment in Annonay, the King asked the Montgolfiers to make a balloon for him. Joseph and Marianne stayed home and Etienne went to Paris to make the balloon. The first one, made for the eyes of the King, was large and decorated with beautiful designs, but there was a rainstorm at its tryout and it was ruined. Etienne hurried to finish another. A young man named Rozier, who helped make the balloon, tried to persuade the King to let him fly with it, but the King refused. On the morning of the flight Rozier finally persuaded the King to let them send up some animals. A sheep, a duck and a rooster were brought from the royal barnyard to the court where the balloon was waiting. They were put into a willow basket which was hitched to the balloon. When the balloon was released, Rozier jumped to his horse and followed it. He found the balloon and its basket in a forest two miles from Paris. The animals were all alive. The sheep was grazing happily, the duck was looking for water but the rooster had an injured wing.

Rozier and a young nobleman named D'Arlandes were the first men to fly. On November 21, 1783, a crowd gathered to watch their ascent, and man's first air voyage began amid the smell of face powder and perfume and the screams and giggles of the ladies of the French court. The two men rose above the rooftops, floating and drifting and controlling their height by feeding or dampening the fire under their paper and cloth balloon. They landed gently five and one-half miles from where they had started.

A BALLOON IS KILLED

The first gas balloon was made by a French professor named Charles. Charles had heard the news of the Montgolfier experiments. He knew of the discovery of hydrogen gas seventeen years before. Hydrogen was and still is the lightest substance known. In those days it was called "inflammable air."

Charles made his balloon of cloth varnished with elastic gum. He made the gas by throwing five hundred pounds of diluted sulphuric acid over one thousand pounds of iron filings.

When Charles released his balloon, Benjamin Franklin was among those who watched it rise. Someone asked Franklin what use a balloon could be.

"And of what use is a newborn baby?" asked Franklin.

The balloon came down in a field near a French village. The people who saw it thought it was a living thing. Some of them ran for their lives, but the braver ones attacked it with their pitchforks and punctured it. The evil smell of the escaping gas made them think that the balloon was a monster from the sky, so they beat it to "death" and tied it to the tail of a horse.

Later, after Charles himself had gone up under a hydrogen balloon, Rozier made a balloon combining a hydrogen gas bag with a cylinder

of hot air. Charles begged him to remember his chemistry. "Do you not know that the gas is inflammable?" he asked.

But in spite of the warning, Rozier and his friend Romain started out to cross the English Channel under the new balloon. Soon after it left the ground the hydrogen caught fire, as Charles had predicted, and Rozier and Romain crashed to the earth.

FIRST IN AMERICA

"What a sight! I thought myself carried on the vows of their hearts." Blanchard grasped his flag in one hand and his cocked hat in the other and waved to the crowd as his balloon steadily ascended. There were people on the roofs of the houses, the steeples, in the streets and on the roads.

In the yard of the Walnut Street Prison in Philadelphia, where the balloon had rested a moment before, a band played and the crowd cheered wildly. George and Martha Washington, Thomas Jefferson, Betsy Ross and a group of American Indians watched with the others. Some of the men jumped on their horses and galloped madly down the road, trying to keep up with the balloon but it grew smaller and smaller and finally disappeared.

A little black dog that a friend had given Blanchard for company tried to get out of the gondola, but finding no landing place, it curled

up at Blanchard's feet. A great flock of pigeons parted when they found the balloon in their path. The Delaware River far below reflected the sunbeams and looked like a white ribbon "no more than four inches wide."

Blanchard reached a height of fifty-eight hundred feet, was aloft forty-five minutes and landed in a field near Woodbury, N.J. The little dog jumped out of the gondola and went straight to a puddle for a drink of water.

Blanchard looked around and saw some men coming toward him. One of them was holding a gun. Blanchard was French and could speak no English but he carried a letter from George Washington, and when he showed the men the letter from their much-loved President they helped him in every way they could. He was taken back to Philadelphia in a coach and on his arrival presented George Washington with the flag which he had carried during the voyage.

Blanchard's ascent, made on January 9, 1793, was the first in America.

Charles Ferson Durant was the first native American balloonist. He made his ascents during the 1820's and 1830's in the interest of science.

DRIFTING WITH THE WIND

You have probably dreamed of how it would feel to flap your arms and fly with the birds. You wouldn't have to worry about airports or fuel. You could go with the wind. Flying in the basket of a balloon is something like that, except that you don't even have to flap your arms. When you leave the ground it seems that the ground is leaving you, and as you drift across the sky you seem to be standing still. The fields and houses and lakes are moving far beneath you. There is no wind because you are part of the wind. Except for the creak of the ropes against the basket it is quiet. Once in a while, almost as if from another world, you might hear the faint sound of a dog barking or a child calling.

In 1804 two scientists, one French and one Russian, made an experimental flight in a balloon. They wanted to take samples of the air, find out how cold it would be, and how they would feel when they were far above the earth. When the earth was a mile and a half below them, the Russian found that by shouting straight down and waiting quietly for ten seconds he could hear clearly the sound of his own voice coming back to him.

They carried bottles filled with liquid and when they were aloft they emptied the bottles and sealed them up again so that they could take air samples back to earth.

They found that the air was colder and thinner as they went higher.

THE LAST OF THE GIANT

Nadar's "Giant" rose over the twinkling lights of Paris in the evening of October 18, 1863. The people in the great basket with its sitting room and sleeping rooms were out for the ride of their lives. By midnight they were drifting over Holland and they could hear the roar of the Zuider Zee. They were afraid that they might come down in the water but a change in the wind took them east. At five o'clock the new day dawned.

One of the voyagers was a young reporter. He wrote that the woods seemed "the size of bouquets." He said that "the villages are so white and clean that I think the Dutch housewives must scour the roofs of their houses every morning. In the midst of every village there is a jewel of a church with a shining steeple."

As the balloon passed over the villages its passengers laughed at the quacking of the ducks, the swearing of the men and the screaming of the women and children below.

They drifted over Germany and looked down to see a steamboat chugging along a river. The sun grew hot and the balloon began to expand and they decided to come down before it exploded. Nadar opened the valve, and everyone climbed the ropes. The balloon dropped much too fast and struck the ground with tremendous force and bounced up again. It crashed again and bounced again. It cut through trees and one of the anchors tore away the roof of a house.

Finally the balloon crashed in a forest. Three of its passengers were seriously injured, but, by a near miracle, nobody was killed.

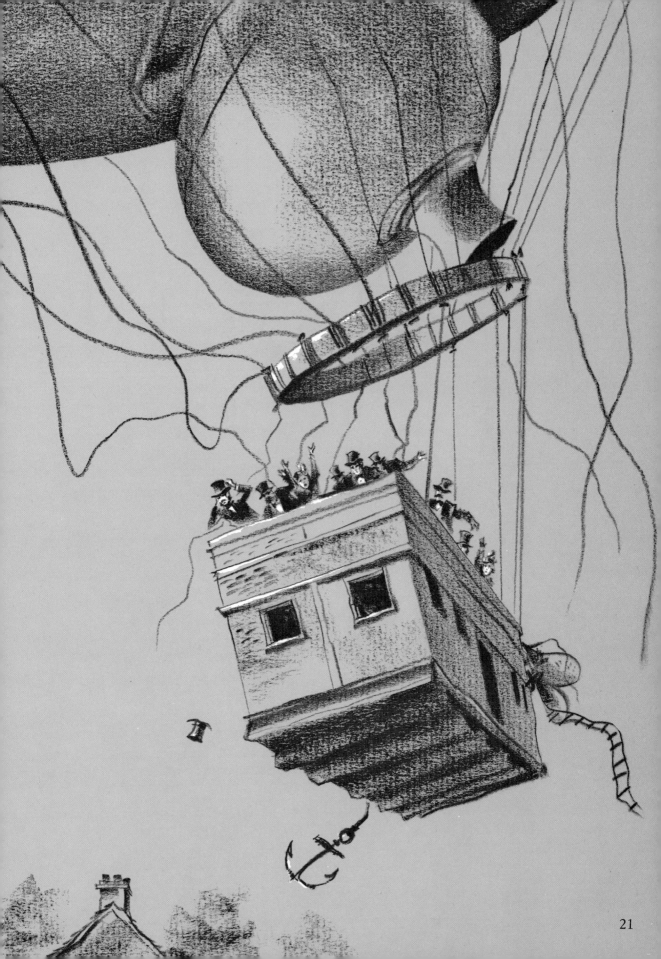

Weddings in the baskets of balloons,
New York 1865, Cincinnati 1874.

In the 1800's, showmen went
up on horseback.

Balloons at the coronation of Napoleon in 1804.

PHOTO FROM *THE FLIGHT OF THE SMALL WORLD*, W. W. Norton Company

"The Small World" in which three men and one woman tried to cross the Atlantic. They ballooned west from the Canary Islands off Africa and came down 1200 miles at sea. They sailed the remaining 1500 miles in their "basket" which was a fifteen-foot sailboat.

Swiss and German balloons at the start of a race. The balloon that lands farthest from the starting point wins.

WIDE WORLD PHOTOS

FUN, SPORT AND ADVENTURE

FROZEN MIST

When he was a boy in Sweden, Andrée's mother wrote that "from the very first moment he opened his eyes to the light of day he has been an uncommonly big and strong child." She noted that his questions were always hard to answer. He was never satisfied until he got to the core of a problem.

He grew up as he had started and it was such a man, curious and adventurous, who planned an unusual polar expedition that ended in his own death and the death of his two friends, Strindberg and Fraenkel.

In 1876 he visited America and worked for a time as a janitor. He met John Wise of Philadelphia who taught him to pilot a balloon.

When he returned to Sweden where he worked as a scientist, he took time to experiment with balloons. One evening while walking with Nordenskjöld, the famous arctic explorer and discoverer of the Northwest Passage, the great man suggested to him the possibility of flying to the North Pole in a balloon.

Andrée designed a balloon that he thought could make the trip. He called it the "Eagle."

On July 11, 1897, the three men, Andrée, Strindberg and Fraenkel, sent up little balloons to test the direction of the wind and agreed the time had come to take off. Strindberg, who was a fine scientist and an expert photographer, wrote later that their departure from their friends was sad but that they shook hands all around "without a sign of weakness."

Not until fifty years later, on a glittering day, were the remains of their last camp found. It was discovered by a Norwegian sealing party on White Island, Spitsbergen, which uncovered diaries and undeveloped film. The film was unharmed and when it was developed it showed, among other things, several pictures of the balloon resting where it had landed on the ice. Andrée and his friends had walked to White Island, pushing their supplies on sleds. The balloon was never found but it is certain that it never reached the Pole.

The picture shows Andrée releasing a carrier pigeon. Only
one of his pigeons was found. It bore the message,
"All well on board. This is third pigeon post."

The picture below was taken by Auguste Piccard from
his steel gondola on his second trip into the stratosphere.
It shows a section of the towering, snow-covered Italian
Alps. It is the first picture ever taken from the stratosphere.

WIDE WORLD PHOTOS

The picture on the opposite page shows Auguste Piccard's
balloon being carried to the starting field in
Augsburg, Germany.

WIDE WORLD PHOTOS

THE PICCARD TWINS

When they were young, Auguste and Jean Felix Piccard took to the air over Switzerland. Once when they were floating in the sky they saw the roof of their own house just below them. They called to their mother and she came out of the house and looked around. When she didn't see them, she went back inside. She had never thought to look up!

When he grew older, Jean Felix came to America to live. Auguste stayed in Europe and he began to dream of a great adventure. He wanted to know more about the stratosphere, the region of cold, thin air above the air we live in. He began to design a balloon that would take him there. He knew that in twenty minutes or half an hour he could reach the stratosphere but that if he went there in an open gondola he would freeze to death or die from lack of air. He built an airtight gondola to attach to a huge balloon.

In Augsburg, Germany, at dawn on May 27, 1931, Auguste and a young man named Paul Kipfer climbed into the gondola and prepared to take off. The balloon rose swiftly and as the air became thinner the gas expanded and the balloon grew rounder. They entered the stratosphere and found themselves in a region where the weather was always calm and beautiful. There were no clouds and there were no snowstorms. A brilliant sun rose over the horizon and moved across a sky so dark that it was almost black.

Auguste studied cosmic rays, which are thought to be made by the breaking up or formation of atoms in outer space. The brilliance of the sun made their cabin feel like an oven. When they finished their experiments, their water was gone and they were thirsty. They had been up a long time, so they pulled the cord

Continued on the next page.

to open the gas valve to bring the balloon to earth, but to their horror they found that the valve was jammed. Now they could do nothing but wait and hope for the best.

When the sun went down and they saw the stars shine more brightly than any man had seen them shine, the balloon cooled and they began to descend. They were to have landed at noon and their families and friends had begun to worry about them.

They found that they were over some of the tallest mountains of Europe. At last, after seventeen hours, they were low enough to open their portholes and take in fresh air. They were still in great danger from the jagged, snowcapped mountains but the air refreshed them. Auguste noted that "The moonlight was magnificent."

Now they were low over glaciers with deep cracks in them. For an instant they saw the lights of a village. Then they saw a glacier that was flat enough for a landing and Kipfer pulled open the ripping panel, letting out all the gas at once. As they landed, Kipfer fell to the floor and everything in the cabin fell on top of him. When Auguste saw the look on his face he laughed until the tears rolled down his cheeks.

They camped where they were, wrapping themselves in the folds of their rubberized cotton balloon. They spent a cold, sleepless night and in the morning they were rescued by mountaineers. They found they had come down near the Tyrolese village of Gurgl.

After that, Auguste made another flight into the stratosphere. This time everything went smoothly and his balloon landed in Italy.

In the meantime Jean Felix was working as a scientist in America. He and his wife Jeannette made a flight into the stratosphere from an airfield in Michigan. During the early part of the flight while Jeannette was on top of the gondola working with the valve rope, her foot slipped and her grip on the rope just saved her from falling. They made a bumpy landing near a pretty country town in the green hills of Ohio. From a scientific point of view their flight was very successful.

MT. WASHINGTON

EMPIRE STATE BUILDING

BASE OF IONOSPHERE   50 MI.
TOP OF STRATOSPHERE

350 MILES TO EXOSPHERE

THE PICCARDS'   40 MI.

PIONEERING

BALLOON

FLIGHTS   30 MI.

For more about earth's atmosphere
read page 48.

                                                       20 MI.

JEAN AND JEANNETTE PICCARD 1934   15 MI.
10.9 MILES   AUGUSTE PICCARD 1932
                                            10.07 MILES
                 AUGUSTE PICCARD 1931
                 9.81 MILES
                                                       10 MI.

BASE OF STRATOSPHERE
TOP OF TROPOSPHERE   5 MI.
                 MT. EVEREST

This old print shows Henri Giffard operating the steam engine of his dirigible balloon in 1852. The gas bag was similar to the one below.

A model of the Tissandier airship which had an electric motor. The airship was built in 1882.

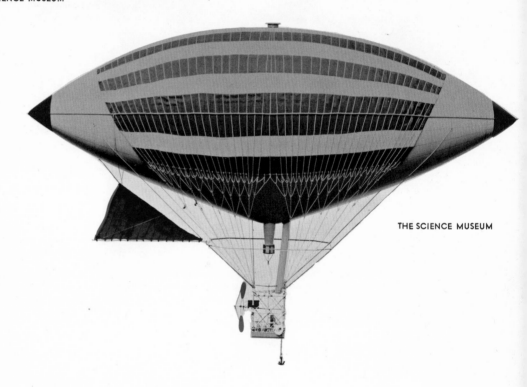

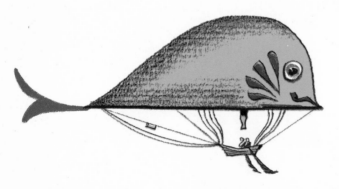

Pauly and Egg's "Dolphin" balloon. People called it "Egg's folly."

On the opposite page is a model of "La France."

EARLY DIRIGIBLES

Almost as soon as balloons were invented men began to try to steer them. The ones shown here were only partly successful. When flying against a strong wind they stood still or went backward. It was hard to steer them, and they could fly for only short distances.

In England in 1816 work was started on a fish-shaped balloon but it was never finished and people laughed at its inventors. A little box between the gondola and the tail was designed to make the balloon go up or down when it was moved forward or back. This idea was used later with some success.

The balloons designed by Henri Giffard and the Tissandier brothers were not powered by engines strong enough to take them against the wind.

During the Civil War an experienced inventor named Dr. Solomon Andrews had amazing success in steering his dirigibles with no engines at all. He had the knack of shifting his weight so that the balloon would go forward but nobody was ever able to explain quite how he did it.

Dr. Andrews made the first flight over New York City. He had difficulty steering that day and when the basket tilted at a crazy angle he and his passengers were nearly spilled into the crowds on Fifth Avenue.

Other airships, such as "La France," built in 1884, were still only partly successful.

THE SCIENCE MUSEUM

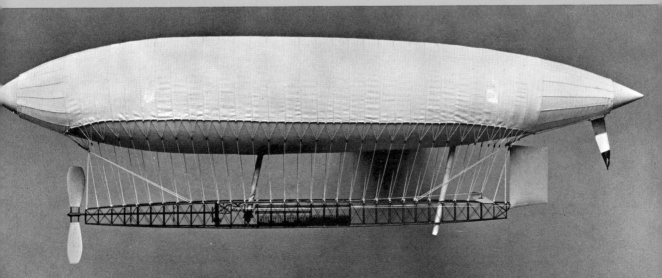

"ARE YOU AFRAID?"

By the time he was twelve Santos-Dumont was driving a big steam locomotive around the sixty miles of track on his family's coffee plantation in Brazil. He flew kites and made countless Montgolfier balloons and watched happily as they floated into the sky. He read about the dirigibles that he believed were to be seen in the skies over Europe.

When he was eighteen he sailed with his family to Paris and found to his great surprise that there were no dirigibles there at all. After learning to pilot a balloon he decided to build a dirigible of his own. He planned to power it with a light gasoline engine. His daring and his flair for invention helped him to succeed where others had failed and his balloons were the first that could really be steered.

On his first dirigible flight his big yellow gasbag began to collapse and he thought he was heading for certain death when he saw some boys playing beneath him. He called to them to grab his guide rope and pull the balloon against the wind. The boys were quick to respond and they saved Santos' life.

With his fifth airship he decided to try for a prize to be given to the first person who would pilot an airship from St. Cloud around the Eiffel Tower and back in thirty minutes. The distance was seven miles and most people thought it could never be done. Santos flew around the tower, but on the way back something went wrong and his balloon was found draped over a tree and the basket dangling above the ground. Santos was sitting in the basket calmly eating his lunch. On his second try his balloon exploded over the rooftops and, just in time to save himself from hurtling into the street, he jumped to a window and hung on for his life.

He built a new airship, a little better than the last, and on September 6, 1901, he tried again. This time he crossed the finish line in twenty-nine minutes and thirty-one seconds and the people cheered him wildly. The men raised him to their shoulders. The women tossed flowers to him and one of them gave him a live white rabbit.

One warm summer day Santos landed his ninth airship at a children's festival. The children crowded around and he gave the closest one a ride. The child was an American boy named Clarkson Potter.

"Are you afraid?" Santos asked him as they rose into the sky.

"Not a bit!" said the boy.

No. 5 explodes.

They called him the "Crazy Count" when he built his first dirigibles but they began to believe in Graf von Zeppelin when he steered and flew his third ship against the wind. His fourth ship was hailed as a triumph but she burned after blowing loose from her moorings in a high wind. All over Germany people heard the news, "The balloon has burned!" Thousands of his countrymen sent him money to build a new ship, and the age of the great rigid dirigibles was born.

Other countries began to build them and their story became one of disaster. The pride of Britain, the "R101," started on a trip to India and burned over France. In the early hours of a Sunday morning she lay half on a field and half over woods like the white skeleton of a huge whale. The "Shenandoah," an American Navy dirigible, broke into three parts in a storm over Ohio. Part of the "Shenandoah" ballooned into the air, and the seven men clinging to it managed to bring it back to earth. Others saved themselves too, but the gondola dropped to earth like a stone. The U.S.S. "Akron" and her sister ship the "Macon" were lost at sea.

WIDE WORLD PHOTOS

The non-inflammable, helium-filled U.S. Navy airship "Macon" which crashed into the Pacific in 1935. She had a hangar which held five planes. One plane can be seen under the ship.

Some of the great airships traveled thousands of miles with no mishap and the "Graf Zeppelin" traveled over a million miles and made a trip around the world.

On a Thursday morning in 1937 children in their schoolyards in Boston looked up and watched the great silver "Hindenburg" moving slowly across the sky. After lunch the passengers looked out of the slanted windows at the dark shadow of their airship rippling across the waters of Long Island Sound. They had no reason to be afraid. The "Hindenburg" was longer than three city blocks and she had crossed the Atlantic many times before. The trip was almost over. The lunch had been good and the chairs were comfortable. The walls were decorated with the designs of early flight. One of them was a picture of the Montgolfier balloon.

The "Hindenburg's" arrival at Lakehurst, N.J., was delayed by the weather but finally she moved toward her mooring mast. Suddenly a small spark danced under the ship and she burst into flames. Terrible fireworks lit the evening sky. Within thirty seconds she was a red-hot wreck. Before she had cooled thirty-three people had died and three more were fatally injured. Some escaped as if by a miracle. A fourteen-year-old cabin boy named Franz Werner ran from the flames, wet but unhurt because a water tank had burst over his head.

No one was sure what has caused the accident but it marked the end of the great rigid dirigibles.

The hydrogen-filled "Hindenburg" seconds after she exploded.

WIDE WORLD PHOTOS

BALLOONS IN WAR

Blimp covering convoy in World War II.
OFFICIAL U.S. NAVY PHOTO

Coutelle stood in front of the general and explained how he thought balloons could be used in war. He explained that they would be useful in finding out the strength and position of the enemy. The general rose from his chair, his face bright red. "Get out of here or I will shoot you!" he said.

Coutelle found another general who would listen, and he organized a French balloon corps which used balloons for the first time in war.

In World War I, observers in balloons towed by ships said that it was as easy to spot a sub from a balloon as to see a fish in a pond.

During World War II barrage balloons, tethered by strong wires, were used over England to keep enemy planes from flying in low to bomb and strafe.

U.S. Navy radar-equipped blimps are used today as part of a system to warn us of enemy attack.

T.S.C. Lowe at the Battle of the Seven Pines during the Civil War.

Barrage balloons over London during World War II. Thousands of these "kite balloons" covered the sky over England.

Coutelle at the Battle of Fleurus, June 26, 1794.

U.S. NAVY

U.S.NAVY

A large plastic balloon being launched ahead of a thunderstorm to study wind conditions in and around the storm. Small plastic balloons are used to make wind studies too. They can be made to drift for hundreds of miles at constant levels.

Launching a weather balloon. The man in the foreground is carrying the radiosonde. The dish-shaped tracking antenna is in the plastic dome.

W. R. GRACE AND COMPANY

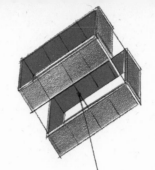

WEATHER BALLOONS

Every day hundreds of balloons go up all over the world. These balloons carry radio transmitters which send back information about the temperature, humidity, barometric pressure and wind speed at various levels. They are called radiosonde balloons.

This information is useful not only in forecasting the weather but it is used by jet pilots to help them decide at what levels to fly. Because their engines take in air, the condition of the air is important to them.

Balloons are sometimes sent into the eyes of hurricanes to help study the structure of these violent storms. When these balloons burst, the instruments are carried safely to earth under bright red parachutes.

Sometimes as many as one thousand balloons are released at once to help people who are studying the speed and direction of the winds. Winds studies are always made before important rocket flights. At high levels, balloons sometimes find wind speeds of over 350 miles an hour. Winds like this would bring disaster to levels where people live.

A weather kite of the kind used in the late 1800's.

Thirty or forty years ago, weathermen plotted the flight of "pilot balloons" with visual instruments.

This photo was taken automatically from the open gondola of Kittinger's balloon two seconds after he left the gondola when he made his first jump. Except that he was not weightless during his pioneering jumps, he experienced pretty much the same conditions that men will experience in outer space when they are outside their space ships. The jumps took place over New Mexico. The photo shows him silhouetted against the White Sands. The San Andreas Mountains are on the right.

40

CAPTAIN KITTINGER U.S.A.F.

In the early hours of a November morning in 1959 Joe Kittinger ate a breakfast of ham and eggs and went to a spot in the New Mexico desert where his ground crew was waiting with the balloon that was to take him into the stratosphere. He had been to the stratosphere before, but this time he was going to jump.

He put on several layers of insulated clothing and lay down and started to breathe pure oxygen. At six-fifteen he climbed into his gondola and the balloon left the earth.

When he was fourteen miles above the earth he stepped out of the gondola. It was cold up there. It was 104 degrees BELOW ZERO. He would have to fall about twelve miles before his parachute opened or he would freeze to death. He dropped like a rock from outer space. He said that at first there was no feeling of movement and no noise; it was like stepping off a porch and landing nowhere. But in about twenty seconds he lost the feeling of stillness and he knew he was falling. He reached a speed of four hundred and fifty miles an hour. Then he began to spin and when he was a little more than two miles from the earth, a barometric device opened his parachute and he drifted slowly to the desert floor.

Jumps like Joe Kittinger's contribute information that will make it easier for men to return to earth from outer space.

When someone asked him if he was afraid when he jumped he said, "Oh, no. It was the quickest way down."

A month after his first jump, Kittinger jumped again. This jump and the ones that came after it were part of project "Excelsior," and both were 100 per cent successful from a medical and scientific standpoint.

Commander Malcolm Ross U.S.N.R. inside the gondola of the "Astronomy Balloon." The gondola was shaped like a ball, and the telescope was mounted on top.

ASTRONOMY BALLOONS

In 1959 Malcolm Ross and Charles Moore rose to a height of sixteen miles in their balloon-borne gondola, which was equipped with a telescope. They went up to study the planet Venus, sometimes called our sister planet. She is closer to earth than any other planet and about the same size. She is surrounded by a dense layer of clouds about two hundred miles thick. Until the flight of Ross and Moore, astronomers thought that there was no water in the atmosphere of Venus, and so they thought there could be no life there.

Ross and Moore had to wait all day in the stratosphere. They shivered so hard that they shook their gondola. Moore said that getting Venus into their sights was like "standing on an icy pond and trying to push a car." Finally at five-fifteen in the morning they got Venus into their sights and obtained the information they wanted.

The telescope and camera are on the truck. Only a small part of the balloon is inflated. The rest stretches along the ground and up to the telescope. Small balloons test wind direction.

Their balloon drifted down over Kansas and the gondola was cut away and brought to earth by a parachute. Now it seemed that the men were safe, but a gust of wind caught the 'chute and the gondola was dragged across the farms of Kansas for half a mile before it was cut loose by U.S. Marines who had been following in helicopters.

The men were badly shaken and their gondola was a wreck, but their findings proved that there is water in the atmosphere of Venus. Is there life there? Maybe there is.

The clearest photographs ever taken of the sun and the planets have been taken from balloons. Our atmosphere, heavy with water and dust, blurs pictures taken from the surface of the earth. From the edge of the atmosphere the moon seems brighter and sharper and the stars and planets don't twinkle as they seem to do when seen from the earth.

An unmanned "Astronomy Balloon" being launched at dawn. This was the flight from which Dr. Martin Schwarzschild obtained the clearest photos ever taken of the sun. They were relayed to earth by TV.

SKYHOOKS

In the Caribbean Sea on a bright day in 1960 a long, silvery, plastic balloon, nearly as tall as a fifty-story skyscraper, towered over the flight deck of the aircraft carrier "Valley Forge." This Navy skyhook balloon "hooked" a load of two thousand pounds. It carried very sensitive photographic plates to record cosmic rays. These rays are believed to hold the secrets of the forces that keep our universe going. Much more is known about them now than was known when the Piccards made their first flights into the stratosphere, but there is much more to be learned.

44

The skyhook was launched in the afternoon and it was tracked by destroyers and planes. It reached a height of more than twenty-two miles. The gondola was released in the afternoon of the following day and was picked up from the water by one of the destroyers. For projects like this, skyhook balloons are better than satellites or rockets because they stay in one area for many hours and can carry a much heavier load.

The photo on the left shows the first Super Skyhook being launched in Minnesota in 1952. Giant unmanned skyhooks are used to carry scientific instruments to high levels. The small balloon helped lift the load at the moment of launch. It was sealed so that it would pop when it rose to where the air was thinner and the pressure less. Jean Piccard designed the first plastic balloons of the skyhook type in 1936.

Skyhook towering over the deck of U.S.S. "Valley Forge."

SPACE BALLOONS

Thousands of people from Maine to the Carolinas got out of their cars and looked in wonder at a huge space balloon that glistened in the light of the evening sun. It was launched by a two-stage rocket from Wallops Island, Virginia, in October of 1959 and inflated in space two hundred and fifty miles above the earth.

To the people who saw it, it looked like a big star with a steady glow and blinking lights around it. Some of them said it twinkled like a Christmas tree. It was the largest—though not the heaviest—object ever put into space. It was not designed to go into orbit. These giant balloons now orbit the earth and are used as reflectors for space communications. Radio and radar signals are bounced off the balloons, making it possible to transmit the signals clearly for thousands of miles.

The picture at left shows the launching of a balloon-carrying rocket. The "smoke" is liquid oxygen.

NASA PHOTO

This picture shows the tip of the rocket with the fairing removed. The metal ball contains the balloon. The ball is blown apart in space and the balloon spills free and inflates automatically. It carries crystals which evaporate and make gas to replace the gas that escapes when the balloon is punctured by meteorites. The balloon is less than the thickness of a human hair.

NASA PHOTO

HOW HIGH IS HIGH?

Before the flights of the Piccards, a friend of theirs named DeBort "discovered" the stratosphere by using sounding balloons. He found that at a height of about seven and one-half miles there was an area where the temperature stayed constant. He called this region the stratosphere.

From fifty to four hundred miles above sea level is the ionosphere, named for "ions" which are electrically charged particles in this area. These particles form a barrier which makes radio and TV broadcasting possible by deflecting radio waves. It is in this area that meteors burn up. The ionosphere acts as a shield protecting us from continuous bombardment from outer space.

In the ionosphere is the auroral region where the northern lights are thought to originate. Above the ionosphere is the exosphere, which continues more than ten thousand miles. In the upper part of the exosphere there is almost no air at all.

As you rise above the earth and the air gets thinner, the sky gets darker. First it turns a deeper blue. It grows deeper and deeper until it starts to take on a violet hue. Then it turns purple and finally it appears to be black. Near the earth it is the light of the sun reflecting on the atmosphere that makes the sky light blue.

This picture shows the first manned flight under a plastic balloon. The flight was made in 1949 by scientist Charles Moore, who is mentioned on page 42. This flight was one of the landmarks in the revival of ballooning as an aid to science. Now all high-level, manned flights are made under these very light, micro-thin balloons.

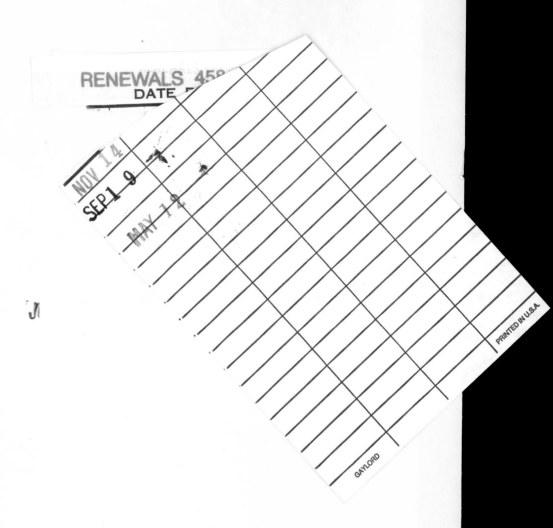